THE ENIGMA OF THE MARGATE SHELL GROTTO

An examination of the theories on its origins

by

Patricia Jane Marsh, M.A.

**Former Director of Studies and Heritage Activities for
The English Cultural Experience Ltd**

CONTENTS

Introduction

The first written record of the existence of the Margate Shell Grotto appeared in a short article published in The Kentish Gazette on 22nd May, 1838. It gave an account of how this underground structure was discovered. Workmen digging in the garden of Belle Vue Cottage on Dane Road had struck a stone slab covering a narrow hole. The hole turned out to be the dome of a *"kind of Aladdin's cave"*, a magnificent complex entirely lined with shells. At the time, the property belonged to a Mr James Newlove, schoolmaster of the Dane House Academy for Boys on the same street. He had started renting Belle Vue Cottage in 1835 and bought it in August 1837. It was both the family home and a girls' school under the direction of Newlove's wife, Arabella.

Ever since the discovery of the Grotto was made public, a large number of theories have been put forward about when, why and by whom this fascinating structure was made. The aim of this booklet is to assess the plausibility of the main contenders in order to reach a tentative conclusion about the likeliest scenario. This is the most that can be achieved unless proof concerning the identity of the builders emerges, or extensive and reliable dating tests are carried out.

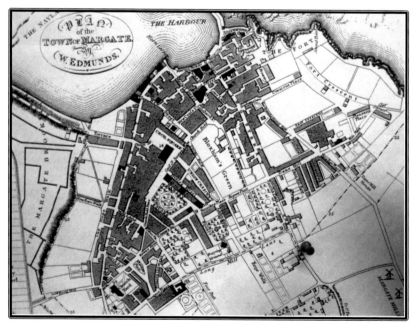

A Town Plan of Margate in 1821

The site of the Shell Grotto is marked with a blue pin in the bottom right-hand section of the map. As can clearly be seen, there were no buildings on the site at this time; the area was open meadowland.

While attempting to assess the plausibility of the various theories concerning the creation of the Margate Shell Grotto, it will be useful to bear in mind **six criteria**. These are:

1. Opportunity

Did the person or people involved in making the structure have the *opportunity* to access the site? Did they own it or live nearby? Could they have worked on it in secret? (No written or oral record of the Grotto existed before 1838. The site itself was open meadowland with no building on it in the 1821 Town Plan.)

2. Motivation

Why was the Grotto built? What was its function or purpose? Why was it kept secret? (There are 2,000 sq.ft (186 m²) of shell mosaic using millions of shells, many of them tiny, quite apart from the labour involved in excavating the passages and chamber. One would expect the creators to have had a good reason for what they did!)

3. Feasibility

Did the person or people involved have the time to build the Grotto, collect the millions of shells and fix them to the walls, or the money to have all these things done? (Scott's Grotto at Ware took thirty years to complete at a rumoured cost of £10,000 and has far less shellwork.)

4. Skills

Did the person or people involved have the skills to excavate the Grotto and/or create the shell mosaic?

5. Construction and Materials

Do the physical characteristics of the Grotto fit with the particular theory under consideration? Such characteristics could include materials and mortars used, source and age of the shells, extent and age of repairs, and likely deterioration according to prevailing environmental conditions.

6. Iconography

Do the shell designs represent subjects typical of the period and/or culture proposed in the theory?

A Former Chalk Pit?

Rod LeGear of the Kent Underground Research Group has drawn attention to the similarity of the shape of the Grotto's dome and surrounding passages to deneholes. These are small mines excavated for the extraction of pure chalk to spread on the fields as fertiliser, a process called 'marling' or 'chalking'. He states that types of denehole with a narrow shaft, as found in the Grotto, usually date from before the

7

Roman occupation to the beginning of the fourteenth century.

LeGear's work throws up the intriguing possibility that the central dome and parts of the passages in the Grotto were originally an abandoned denehole which was extended and decorated with shells at a later date. Such sites were unfortunately not marked on maps, but a certain Mark Holtum (or Holton) claimed, after the existence of the Grotto became known, that he had *"picked the chalk out of"* it.

Two local boys who knew the area well in the 1820s and 1830s were interviewed as elderly gentlemen by the husband of the then Grotto owner, Mr A. G. Goddard. One of them supported the chalk digger's statement, but confusingly commented he had never seen any chalk excavations on the site, which was clearly visible from the road before the house was built. The other stated categorically that there was no chalk pit in that specific location when they were young, although there was a working limekiln in the vicinity. Their evidence tends to indicate that, if the Grotto was indeed originally a denehole, it was extended and decorated prior to the early nineteenth century. Any toolmarks which might help to date the structure are, of course, concealed beneath the plaster and shellwork. Although the pointed shape of the passages has led some commentators to consider them medieval Gothic or nineteenth-century neo-Gothic, LeGear notes that this particular profile was required to support the roof due to the loose-jointed nature of the chalk; serious falls would otherwise have occurred.

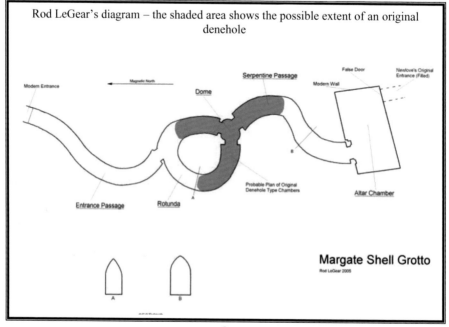

Rod LeGear's diagram – the shaded area shows the possible extent of an original denehole

Modern Entrance

Magnetic North

Dome

Serpentine Passage

False Door

Newlove's Original Entrance (Filled)

Modern Wall

Probable Plan of Original Denehole Type Chambers

Altar Chamber

Entrance Passage

Rotunda

A

B

Margate Shell Grotto

Rod LeGear 2005

19th-Century Claims & Suppositions

The Bowles Brothers

In 1951 a Mrs Elizabeth Jarrett wrote to the Curator and Committee of Ramsgate Museum and to the Mayor of Margate in 1955 about the creation of the Shell Grotto. She claimed that her great-grandfather, Thomas Bowles, had told the owner, James Newlove, as soon as its discovery had been made public, that he and his two elder brothers had built it. They had lived with their widowed mother *"at the cottage opening to within about three feet of the Margate Grotto entrance"*. According to Mrs Jarrett, her own mother claimed the Bowles brothers had first sketched the shell designs on slabs or slates, which she had seen at Thomas Bowles's house. Mrs Jarrett talks about the brothers' sister, Anne, and believes that the cottage next to the Grotto has since been knocked down, although she had visited it herself seventy-three years previously (c.1878). She also thought she remembered hearing that the *"square cavern"* in the Grotto (the 'altar chamber' in Fig.1 on p.8 and on the postcard below) could already have been in use for food storage.

Barbara Jones in Subterranean Britain quotes Mrs Jarrett's account of Thomas Bowles as a child using a little cart to transport shells to the site. In Follies and Grottoes the same author shows a family tree provided by Mrs Jarrett in the 1950s. It claims that Thomas's elder brothers, George and Austen, did the shellwork and *"went to America c. 1812, blocking up the grotto when they left Margate"*.

Old postcard showing the west end of the 'altar' chamber

Christopher Pearson, researcher and Archivist of the Friends of the Shell Grotto, has since established from parish records that there is no trace of anyone named Bowles in Margate who could be part of this family until a certain George Bowles gives his residence as Margate on the occasion of his marriage in Staple in 1819. This person subsequently appears to have lived in Sandwich, where his first son, also called George, was born in 1819 and his second son, John, in 1822. Since his children's birth entries show George Bowles's profession to have been that of a bricklayer, it seems likely that he was lodging in Margate before his marriage, taking advantage of the work generated by the building boom in the town while it was still a fashionable resort.

Belle Vue Cottage (now Rose Lodge), completed by George Bowles in 1834

A Mr Bowles then appears in the Margate Rate Book in July 1824, paying a small amount for a house with no address as yet but in the area of the Grotto field (as subsequent Rate Books testify when the area became more built up). He is recorded as having an additional house and land in December 1829. Unfortunately, no initials are provided to enable us to identify George with absolute certainty, but we know that he built Belle Vue Cottage on land which includes the Grotto underground, bought from John Stroud for a total of £78 in 1829. Various sources refer to the fact that, prior to the purchase, he lived in a small cottage, but it is clear that this was not the family home portrayed in Mrs Jarrett's account. Thomas Bowles, who told Newlove and others that he had made the Grotto with his brothers, was a weaver and ropemaker. He was also Master of the St Lawrence Parish Poorhouse and lived on

Newcastle Hill (now part of Ramsgate) between 1827 and 1835.

George's wife, Anne (perhaps confused with his sister by Mrs Jarrett?), died in 1833 and was buried in St John's churchyard. It was the following year when George sold the land and house he had built and boarded ship with his four sons for America, arriving on 8th December 1834 on the ship President. His elder brother Austen (Augustine) joined him there at some point, or was perhaps already there; George is listed as a brickmason and Augustine as a miller in the 1840 census in Hinsdale, Massachusetts, USA.

Thus, the dates given by Mrs Jarrett appear to be out by some twenty years. She seems to have received a somewhat garbled account of her family history third-hand. It is also worth noting that, as far as we know, George and Austen Bowles never wrote from America to substantiate any claim to making the Shell Grotto, or built any such structures in their new homeland.

Nevertheless, there is one interesting footnote to the story. A 2009 report on the Grotto by the St Blaise building conservation firm found that *"some of the more intricate decorative panels would most probably have been constructed off-site on pieces of slate. These would have been incorporated into the decorative scheme at a later date when required."* This reminds us that Mrs Jarrett mentioned the Bowles brothers first working out the shell designs on slate.

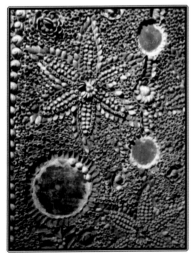

Slate roundels are visible in some damaged panels of the Grotto.

In the middle of the nineteenth century, Charles Knight published an article on Margate in his series <u>The Land We Live In</u>. He states that it was then clear that the Grotto had been made by an *"ingenious artisan"*, who had gone to America. Clearly Thomas Bowles's claims had filtered through to a wider public after all. In later accounts, the whole story appears to have been forgotten; perhaps it had been discounted or disproved by then. It only reappears in the South Eastern Gazette of 15th January, 1924, the sources being again Mrs Jarrett and her great-aunt, Mary Hannah Bowles. Among a large number of inaccuracies, the article claims that the Bowles brothers were unmarried when they made the Grotto (George was certainly married); it also states that they took their inspiration from ancient churches in the area.

Captain Easter and Fanny Schmidt

Another theory about the Grotto concerns a Captain Easter, who had Chateau Belle Vue mansion and pleasure gardens built near its location (on what is now the west side of Wilderness Hill, between about Clifton Place and Dane Road). The boundary wall can still be seen at the end of Grotto Gardens. Records show that Easter began paying rates on his house and land in 1825. As noted above, Margate was a fashionable sea-bathing resort for the upper classes and the wealthy at the time; the Captain was not the first to provide pleasure gardens for the entertainment of tourists.

Chateau Belle Vue in an old print

Fanny Schmidt, the daughter of James Newlove, the first owner of the Grotto, claimed in a letter to A. G. Goddard, a later owner, that her brother had been prompted to look for something underground on the property by a comment to her father by Captain Easter and his friend, a Mr da Costa, that there was something valuable under the land and that Newlove should buy it instead of leasing it. By this time, the Captain had put his mansion and pleasure gardens up for sale.

This statement of Fanny Schmidt's has led to another plausible theory about the Grotto: namely that Captain Easter discovered a pre-existing structure under the land neighbouring his property. He stripped the walls in a search for valuable artefacts or treasure, and then had the shell panels restored, probably by George Bowles, helped by his brother.

As an elderly lady, Fanny Schmidt claimed that her own brother Joshua had discovered the Grotto prior to the event reported in the newspaper, and that he and she had played there with friends, without their parents' knowledge. The entrance had been via a narrow passage, along which they had to crawl. This was apparently the current entrance passage, which their father, James Newlove, had heightened and widened for visitors. We know that he started renting the property in 1835 and that the lease which was never signed (perhaps because Newlove decided to

12

buy the property after his conversation with Easter and da Costa) is preserved in the Grotto archives and is dated February 1835. Fanny stated that Joshua discovered the Grotto during the summer after this conversation, but that he kept it secret from their strict father. She also wrote in her letter to Goddard that the discovery event reported in the newspaper in May 1838 "really" took place in 1837, the year her father bought the property.

Whatever the truth of the matter, work on the structure was certainly carried out after Newlove discovered it; two schoolboys at the Boys' Academy reported that they collected shells from the beach for the purposes of repair. One of them thought that part of the structure may have been bare of shells, but was understandably vague on the subject, since his interview, like Fanny Schmidt's, took place sixty years after the event.

There have been several claims that the end chamber, at least, was dug out and decorated with shellwork in the nineteenth century. These are based on the diary comment of Miss L. S. Daniell after her visit to the Grotto in 1844. She writes that *"since it has been known, a circuitous passage has been cut into the rock to descend into it, **and at the farther end a large room has been excavated and similarly ornamented**".*

Analysis of Nineteenth-Century Claims

If we apply the **criteria** set out on p.7 to these theories of a nineteenth-century date for the Grotto, we can quickly establish that the Bowles hypothesis satisfies the first and perhaps fourth ones: George Bowles owned the property for five years and so had the opportunity to build the Grotto; he was, moreover, a bricklayer, so may well have had the skills to excavate and decorate the structure.

Turning to our fifth criterion, the materials used point to a nineteenth-century construction of the Grotto. The mortar samples taken from the front of five panels and analysed for the 2009 St Blaise report turned out to be of various kinds, but all only produced after 1796. Another set of mortar samples taken in 1999 from different sites were not, however, dated in this way. No firm conclusions can be drawn from these analyses. We know that repairs were carried out by Newlove before the Grotto was opened to the public in 1838; these may have been extensive. It is also a recorded fact that shells have constantly had to be replaced owing to the activities of souvenir hunters. Consequently, it is not surprising that different nineteenth-century mortars have been found on the front of panels easily accessible to visitors.

If we are to date the Grotto definitively from mortar samples, a large number will need to be collected from much less accessible locations.

13

Looking up part of the serpentine passage. Could such intricate designs requiring millions of shells have been created by candlelight in a few years by a 19th-century bricklayer, his only access to the site being to crawl down a narrow passage?

The end chamber of the Grotto is said to have had a vaulted ceiling, which was removed when the owner had an extension to the house on the site built over this area. The inward curving around the edges of the plaster in the chamber certainly gives weight to this assertion. According to Adrian Powell, a stone conservator and archaeologist who has worked on the Grotto, there is evidence that the foundations for the extension intruded on the original fabric of this part of the underground structure and repairs then had to be made around the chamber entrance.

The archway with its decorative keystone in the end chamber is clearly not part of the original construction – there is a rounded-arch doorway visible behind it. Powell has dismissed the idea that this archway could have been installed to support the ceiling but confirmed that it is nineteenth-century. The most logical conclusion is that it masks damage done to the doorway when the foundations for the extension were built.

Interestingly, the only place where foreign shells are found in the Grotto is here – a queen conch from the Caribbean in two corners of the plastered ceiling and giant clams from the Indo-Pacific over the niche and the entrance arch. We know from Harper Cory's work, The Goddess at Margate, that the niche was explored in the late 1940s by the then owner, Charles E. Mitchell. It seems likely that the pattern of the keystone created by the clams was made when the niche was restored after this or an earlier intervention. The shellwork in this section was below the standard of much of the rest of the Grotto before recent restoration.

The important point to make here is that the keystone pattern considered by John Newman in <u>North East and East Kent</u> (Pevsner series) to be the *"tell-tale feature"* marking the whole Grotto out as nineteenth-century is almost certainly a later addition, and tells us nothing about the age of the structure as a whole.

The archway in the end chamber is a nineteenth-century addition (the original doorway is clearly visible behind it).

Descendants of Thomas Bowles claimed to have seen slabs or slate panels with designs on them at his house in Ramsgate. It has now been established that small roundels of slate were used as a base for parts of the Grotto shell mosaic. The current owners of the site have started a project to repair the damaged ones and commissioned a conservator to recreate the mosaic. However, another recent project established that the shellwork was coming away from the chalk surface; the support for the mosaic has been repaired as far as possible. Many irregularities were revealed in the walls; indeed, there may be cavities and even further passages behind the shellwork. Be that as it may, we can safely conclude that most of the shell mosaic was applied to a layer of mortar on the walls and ceilings, definitely not stuck to slabs or large slate panels installed in the underground passages and chamber.

Moreover, the nineteenth-century theory falls down on the second, third and sixth criteria we established. *Why* would George Bowles make such a structure with its huge expanse of the most intricate and elaborate shellwork in the country and not open it to the public, especially as he had a large mortgage to pay off on the property?

Then there is the feasibility aspect: it is claimed that the structure was excavated and decorated by the Bowles brothers at the same time as a house was being built on the site. The millions of shells required would have taken years to collect and much time and effort to transport. The mussels, cockles, whelks, oysters and scallops used throughout the Grotto could have been found along the North and North-East Kent coast – from Shell Ness on the Isle of Sheppey to Shell Ness in Pegwell Bay; they have been harvested in the area for food for millennia.

However, the millions of tiny flat winkle shells used for the vast areas of background between designs have always been rare locally. They are also not used for food or in any manufacturing process. These shells were brought to Margate from beaches west of Southampton, perhaps for their intense orange and yellow colours.

The most serious objection to an early nineteenth-century date for the Grotto relates to the iconography, which cannot be seen to fit the period. Alongside innocuous – though clearly exotic – plants and flowers, there are the strangest of shell designs which do not appear to represent anything, and are certainly not recognisable as typical British or European patterns from the period, or similar to anything used in other grottoes of the time. They have three-pointed stars, elaborate lozenges and what appears to be a plant with eyes in an elongated head. If they were made in the last two hundred years, indeed at any time in our recorded history, we could expect to find parallel images with which we could compare them. Furthermore, no resemblance to the decoration of ancient churches, claimed as inspiration in the 1924 article, is evident.

Indeed, it is this lack of iconography similar to that of the Grotto which lies at the heart of the Margate puzzle.

Panel 21   Panel 50
Two of the strange panels in the Grotto which have no known parallels

The Buddha

One footnote to the nineteenth-century associations of the Margate site is the presence of a figurine of the Buddha, identified as such in 1908 by Sir Francis Younghusband, a former British Commissioner to Tibet. It was attached to the wall above Panel 50, but by 1951 the statuette had been removed, apparently in an act of vandalism.

The Buddha lived in the 5th century BCE in the Indian sub-continent, and Christian tradition claims that the writings of St Origen in the 3rd century stated that Buddhism had come to Britain five hundred years earlier through missionaries of the Emperor Ashoka Maurya.

Before we jump to the conclusion that the Shell Grotto could have been made by Ancient Buddhists, it is important to note that no mention of the figurine above Panel 50 has as yet been found before 1885, when Marie Correlli, a popular Victorian novelist visiting the site, describes *"the small figure of a man in a sitting posture, carved out of one stone; the arms are tightly folded, the head is gone, but judging from the position of the body, the head had evidently turned downwards so that the chin rested on the breast"*.

If this statuette had been present when the Grotto was first opened to visitors, it would surely have been mentioned in an account from that time, situated as it was in such a prominent position above the first panel facing the visitor on entering the Grotto. It therefore appears much more likely that the Buddha figurine was placed above this important panel much later in the 19th century. In 1879 Sir Edwin Arnold compiled an epic poem, "The Light of Asia", describing the Buddha's life, and the Pāli Text Society was founded in 1881 by Thomas William Rhys Davids to foster and promote the study of the Buddhist scriptures, written in Pāli. The lower section of Panel 50 is thought by some to represent a sea turtle; the Buddha used this creature to illustrate *"the precious rarity of opportunity afforded by our human birth"*.

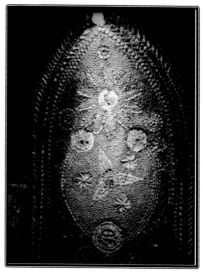

The exposed plaster at the top of Panel 50 shows where the figurine stood.

Late-nineteenth-century followers of the Buddha may well have considered the figurine an appropriate addition to this panel in the Grotto.

18th-Century Origins?

Lady Holland

Shell grottoes were built in Europe from the fifteenth century onwards. They were based on the Renaissance fashion for Classicism and were made for gentlemen and ladies of wealth and learning as places of contemplation. Many were created in Britain in the eighteenth century by wealthy aristocrats returning from their Grand Tour of Europe. They invariably followed Classical themes of nymphs, sea gods and maritime creatures, usually incorporating a water feature and sometimes a cave. There is documented evidence about their building and most of them were made as a rich man's folly, a public display of wealth.

Headley & Meulenkamp in their book Follies - Grottoes & Garden Buildings favour Georgina Caroline, Lady Holland, daughter of the Duke of Richmond, as the creator of the Margate Grotto. Her mother, Sarah, Duchess of Richmond, decorated a shell room with her daughters at

Goodwood in West Sussex during the 1740s. They used shells brought by ship from all over the world and created mainly floral and star patterns with them. As can be seen from the photograph below, the decoration is restrained and highly Classical – nothing in the least comparable to that of the Margate site.

© Clive Boursnell
Section of the shell room at Goodwood - the Classical style
is clearly different from that of the shell panels in Margate

Lady Holland's husband, Henry, Lord Holland, built a series of follies at Kingsgate, three miles along the coast from Margate, during the 1760s. These consisted of Kingsgate Castle, Neptune's Temple, two towers and an arch. After excavating a tumulus in the area, he believed it to have been the site of a battle in the ninth century between Saxons and Danes.

Headley & Meulenkamp go so far as to accuse previous owners of the Margate Grotto of destroying any evidence connecting it with the Hollands. In fact, public records show that the open fields above the Grotto were owned from 1755 by a Beaton Cowell. The land seems to have stayed in the family until about 1821, when a John Cowell left the land to his widow, Elizabeth Crouch Cowell, to divide up and sell as building plots. Needless to say, there was no mention anywhere of an underground structure beneath the land. The next information we have is that John Stroud sold George Bowles two plots in 1829; these became the site of Belle Vue Cottage and that of the Grotto. So, applying our first criterion to the theory that the Hollands had the Shell Grotto built in Margate, there was no opportunity for them to do so, since they did not own the land.

Nevertheless, in <u>Subterranean Britain</u> Barbara Jones claims that *"common sense and the look of the thing itself"* indicate it was made in the late eighteenth century or the very early nineteenth. In <u>Follies and Grottoes</u> she claims *"reasonable writers"* agree with this. Yet is it really common sense or reasonable to claim that a structure of such size and intricacy, which logic dictates must have taken years – if not decades – to complete, was created in secret under a field? As stated earlier, follies of the period were built by wealthy people for show. Secrecy on the part of the person who had this 'folly' built would rather defeat the purpose. It simply defies reason to leave the most impressive creation of them all in England hidden away in a nondescript location. The Hollands certainly did not hide any of their follies at Kingsgate.

Jones's argument also fails on *"the look of the thing itself"*. Perhaps she was referring to the images of flowers, urns and stars common to most grottoes, since there are none of the usual statues, maritime motifs, wreaths or other designs typical of eighteenth-century structures of the type. Yet in Margate the frequently occurring themes are executed in a flamboyant style bearing little resemblance to Classicism. It should also be remembered that flowers, stars and urns with plants growing out of them have all been represented in the most ancient human civilisations we know: on Malta, in Egypt and Mesopotamia. Moreover, the panels which are unique to the Margate site are numerous. It is also worth noting that eighteenth-century grotto builders appear to have vied with each other in using the most exotic shells from far-flung places. In contrast, the Margate Grotto panels are made with the humblest of shells: winkles, cockles, mussels, oysters and whelks.

An alcove in the Hampton Court House shell grotto, completed c. 1769, a typical 18th-century structure with a Classical theme. The shells in this alcove are clearly exotic and the design bears no resemblance to that of the Margate Grotto.

(Photo by Squirmelia, www.flickr.com)

A Margate Hellfire Club?

Some visitors to the Shell Grotto have compared it with the West Wycombe chalk caves extended in the 1750s by order of Sir Francis Dashwood, the notorious founder of the Knights of St Francis of Wycombe, later known as the Hellfire Club. These consist of a series of chambers linked by long narrow passages stretching a quarter of a mile underground. The entrance is via a church-like façade. Meetings of the Club sometimes took place there in its dying days and seem to have consisted of pagan rituals and feasting, reputedly culminating in orgies.

The Margate Grotto mainly consists of narrow passages under a field only reached by crawling along a narrow tunnel; this would not make it ideal for even the slimmest of aristocrats and ladies to desport themselves in the ways described. One also wonders how a banqueting table and couches could have been transported into the chamber.

Alexander Pope's Grotto?

The theory should also be mentioned here that the shell-lined walls of one of the best-known eighteenth-century grottoes were actually transported in blocks to Margate and concealed under the field. This idea is elaborated in Ruby Haslam's Reality and Imagery and refers to Alexander Pope's Grotto at Twickenham. Apart from the fact that the description of the shellwork there does not correspond to what we see at Margate, it is now clear that, except for a number of slate roundels, the majority of the mosaic has been applied directly to the chalk walls (see p.16), not fixed on stone slabs which have been attached to the chalk.

Haslam's theory also fails on other criteria: the opportunity is lacking, the motivation is weak (Could the shellwork not have been preserved on the premises of one or other of Pope's admirers rather than under a field in Margate?) and the iconography bears no relation to the known Classical and religious themes of Pope's Grotto.

The Tudor Hypothesis

Several people feel that the designs incorporating plants in the Grotto are reminiscent of Tudor work, spectacular enough to have graced a mansion like Hampton Court Palace. This is certainly true, but we again come up against the 'problem' panels; they bear no relation whatsoever to Tudor design. As Gerald Moody of the Trust for Thanet Archaeology stated, it is to be hoped that one day a letter from the sixteenth century will be discovered, detailing a visit by some dignitary to a wondrous underground grotto in the town of Margate. Until then, there is no supporting evidence for the Tudor hypothesis.

An embroidered Tudor nightcap with floral designs reminiscent of some Grotto panels

It is worth mentioning here, however, that radiocarbon dating was carried out in 1963 of a fragment of the shell mosaic from the east wall of the Grotto chamber, damaged by a bomb during the Second World War and subsequently replaced with bare plaster. It was done by the University of California at Los Angeles (UCLA), a well-respected laboratory at the time, and the results were published in the journal Radiocarbon (1963) Vol. 5, p.19. In layman's terms, they date the piece to any time between 1570 and 1770. (The Tudor period began in 1485 and ended in 1603.)

However, Dr Gordon T. Cook, Professor of Environmental Geochemistry at the SUERC Radiocarbon Dating Laboratory in East Kilbride, states that these results would now be considered very imprecise, although there is no reason to doubt the measurement. Re-calibrated with modern methodology, it would mean the piece dated to any time between 1710AD and the mid-1950s.

The Knights Templar Claim

There have been assertions that the Margate Grotto is one of the sites in Europe connected with the Knights Templar. As many will be aware, the Knights Templar were members of a Christian military monastic order set up in the eleventh century to protect pilgrims on their way to Jerusalem. It is claimed that they built and/or tended a number of sites in Europe on certain latitudes, and that these locations form part of a secret map, similar to a chart of ley lines.

Michael Twyman's research (2006) dates the Grotto's shellwork to the fourth century BCE. He believed the site was dedicated to the Earth Goddess and aligned to the solstices and equinoxes. He reached these conclusions after taking measurements of various angles in the panels and after observation of the position of the sun projected onto the inside of the dome. Twyman considered that the end chamber was added by the Templars in medieval times (1141 CE). Certain features of its design suggest it was used for the Masonic rituals they practised.

The shell mosaic in the Margate Grotto contains no overt Christian symbols or representations of Middle Eastern monsters commonly portrayed in medieval churches and associated with the Templars. Since Twyman's theories hinge on hidden features and disputed symbols, they await the corroboration of more convincing and unambiguous evidence.

An Ancient Ceremonial Site?

This brings us to those who have proposed a prehistoric date for the Shell Grotto's origins.

Could the Grotto have been some kind of temple?

If the site cannot be shown to date from the time when such structures were most fashionable, in the eighteenth century, then it might date from Antiquity, when it would have been built as a shrine or place of worship. The Grotto has been attributed to Minoans, Hindus, Aztecs or Mayans, among others. It is certainly true that individual shell panels have echoes of these cultures, but none of them can account for the overall imagery of the structure. Moreover, all these theories suffer from the same problem *vis á vis* our criteria: history and archaeological finds in Margate do not support an opportunity for these cultures to have been present on this island and to have built an underground structure.

The cultures concerned were also little known in the early nineteenth century; it is unlikely that a builder of the Grotto at that time would have imitated their art.

The Romans

This part of England was, of course, part of the Roman Empire for more than three-and-a-half centuries (43 CE - c. 410 CE). There are several Roman sites on the Isle of Thanet which have been excavated, including a villa in Margate. Roman soldiers with time on their hands could well have spent it creating the Grotto. The Comprehensive Gazetteer of England and Wales 1894-5 is of the opinion that the structure *"seems most probably to be of Roman origin"*. However, we have already pointed out that the Margate Grotto bears no resemblance to the Classical structures representing nymphs and sea gods copied from Roman times by the fashionable elite of eighteenth-century England.

Another theory connected with the Romans is that the Grotto is a Mithraic temple. The cult of the god Mithras was especially popular among Roman soldiers. The Encyclopaedia Britannica tells us that these temples were artificial grottoes, built wholly or partially underground, to imitate mountain caves in Asia, where the cult originated. They were orientated North-South, like the Shell Grotto. Yet all known Mithraic temples show the god Mithras slaying a bull. There were also long, built-in tables and often benches for the banquets which were held as part of the rites. Both vital elements of the god slaying the bull and the banqueting tables are absent in the Grotto. The Mithraic theory appears to lack plausibility on architectural as well as iconographical grounds.

| Mithras and the bull, fresco from Temple of Mithras, Marino, Italy, 2nd century CE | Bible Museum in Nijmegen. Roman town: reconstruction (artist's impression) of a Mithras temple |

The Phoenicians

There is one other theory dating the Grotto to Antiquity which appears to satisfy our criteria rather more convincingly. Howard Bridgewater, author of <u>The Grotto</u>, considered that the Margate site was built by the Phoenicians during the second half of the first millennium BCE.

It has long been said that the Isle of Thanet, on which Margate lies, was used by the Phoenicians as a trading post when shipping tin from Cornwall to the Continent. Indeed Ayllet Sammes, a scholar from

Christ's College, Cambridge, writing in 1676, derived the ancient name of the Roman province of Britannia from the Phoenician word *Bratanac*, or *Barat-anac* ('Country of Tin').

'Phoenician' is actually the Greek name for the people who inhabited the land which roughly corresponds today to the territory of Lebanon. They referred to their own language as Canaanite; it closely resembled Ancient Hebrew. D. R. J. Perkins, director for many years of the Trust for Thanet Archaeology, quotes experts in the field who *"speculate that there was an extensive Carthaginian trading network rounding Thanet to the Thames estuary, East Anglia and Lincolnshire"*. The Carthaginians were Phoenicians who set up a colony in Carthage, North Africa, in the thirteenth century BCE.

Bridgewater has another agenda in claiming the Grotto is the work of Phoenicians; he does not provide direct evidence from Margate to support his claim. However, while investigating this theory, a number of elements which lend it significant credence were unearthed.

The first concerns etymology. A strong contender for the origin of the name of the Isle of Thanet is the Phoenician goddess, Tanit. Professor Theo Vennemann, a specialist in historical linguistics and etymology, is persuasive in showing the derivation of Thanet from Tanit and revealing problems with the Celtic origin proposed earlier.

Vennemann also draws attention to the fact that in Gadir (Cadiz), a Carthaginian/Phoenician colony on an offshore island similar to Thanet, there was an oracle cave – an interesting parallel with our mysterious underground structure in Margate. Linguistically speaking, it would also be possible to derive the name Margate from the Phoenician god, Melqart, but the current lack of any reference to the place prior to the thirteenth century makes it difficult to support this hypothesis historically. The same is true of the Isles of Sheppey and Grain off the North Kent coast further west; if Thanet is named after Tanit, perhaps they were named for Shapash, goddess of the sun, and Yam, god of the sea.

Let us move on to more supporting evidence about the Phoenicians. According to Professor Maria Evgenia Aubet, author of <u>The Phoenicians and the West</u>, *"the Phoenicians established themselves on islands and islets, peninsulas and coastal promontories with good natural anchorages, bays and inlets sheltered from the winds and currents, easy to defend against possible dangers from the sea or the mainland and situated at the mouths of rivers or natural access routes to the interior of the territory."* This description would identify Margate as an ideal location for the Phoenicians. It was in a sheltered position on the

Isle of Thanet, an offshore island in Ancient Times. There was even a creek running into the sea at Margate, although it has disappeared as a result of the considerable changes in the topography of the island over the centuries, which have made it part of the mainland for at least the last three hundred years.

Moreover, the Phoenicians tried to keep their trading posts secret from competitors such as the Greeks, and later the Romans, in order to maintain their commanding position as the foremost merchants of the era. The Greek geographer Strabo relates the story of a Phoenician captain heading into dangerous 'shoal water' rather than leading a Roman vessel to his destination, the Cassiterides (the tin mines of Cornwall or of the Isles of Scilly). Both ships were wrecked, but the captain was apparently well compensated by the Phoenician state for his losses.

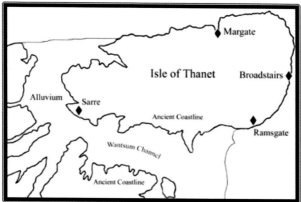

Map of Isle of Thanet in Ancient Times
(reproduced here by kind permission of the Trust for Thanet Archaeology)

There is evidence of human occupation in the Margate area from the Neolithic period, the Bronze Age and the Iron Age; no identifiably Phoenician artefacts have been unearthed anywhere on Thanet to date. Nevertheless, we must bear in mind that the coastline around Margate has been considerably eroded since prehistoric times. David Scurrell in The Book of Margate quotes an observed rate of attrition of thirty metres per century. This would mean that the remains of any Phoenician/Carthaginian trading post from the middle of the first millennium BCE could now lie under the sea, 750 metres from the present coastline. The ruins of a man-made structure are visible at low tide off Foreness Point east of Margate, and two underwater features in Margate Bay, tentatively identified as groynes, are marked in an archaeological survey. These would all be the remains of much more recent building. The possibility of a small Phoenician settlement now far out to sea in this area should not be completely discounted.

Scurrell also comments: *"But for the fact that most of Margate was built over before excavations were carried out in the modern scientific way, probably much more evidence of these early periods would have been found."* There are persistent rumours on Thanet that a large number of children's bones were found by workmen digging foundations in the 1980s; fearing that construction would be severely delayed if they revealed this to archaeologists, they reburied the bones and continued with the building. It is known that the Carthaginians carried out child sacrifice, although in Carthage this was done by fire and the cremated remains stored in an urn. I cite this reputed incident of the finding of children's bones, however, to highlight the fact that we are mostly ignorant of what lies beneath our feet.

Nevertheless, four of the Late Bronze Age skeletons found at the site of a cemetery used sporadically for a millennium or more at Cliffs End on the Isle of Thanet, south of Margate, have been shown to be of individuals from the Western Mediterranean area. The ruins of the Phoenician colony of Carthage lie near Tunis on the North African coast in the Western Mediterranean and the Carthaginians had a number of colonies throughout the region.

Furthermore, the Romans are known to have destroyed anything they found of their Phoenician enemies (by then based in Carthage), melting down their coins, for example, with the result that few have been found. Yet the high concentration of those which *have* been unearthed in Britain in what is now East Kent (far south-east corner of the country) provides yet more evidence suggesting Carthaginians had a presence there.

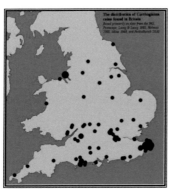

Map by Dr Caitlin Green showing the distribution of Carthaginian coins found in Britain

If the Shell Grotto was a Phoenician/Carthaginian structure, its entrance may have been blocked and sealed before the Romans appeared on the Isle of Thanet in the first century CE. On the other hand, it may have been venerated by the Romans, or at least regarded as a sacred place. The area has long been known as Lucas Dane. Twyman (2002) notes that *lucus* is the Latin for a sacred grove.

But let us return to Melqart, the Phoenician god who may have given his name to Margate. The name itself means 'King of the City'. A temple was always erected to him first in any new colony because business was conducted under his auspices and oaths sworn in his name. The famous Pillars of Hercules, which once marked the exit from the Mediterranean into the Atlantic Ocean, were probably the huge columns of the Temple of Melqart at Gadir (Cadiz). The Greeks translated Melqart's name into their own Heracles and the Romans into Hercules.

If Margate was a Phoenician trading post, if only a small one, there should be traces of a temple to Melqart. But East Kent is well known for its lack of building stone – the fine creamy stone used for Canterbury Cathedral comes from Caen in Normandy. This gives the Phoenicians a valid reason for making a temple and/or oracle to their principal god in Margate underground.

By some accounts, Melqart was also King of the Underworld and was certainly associated with the cycle of vegetation. It might seem appropriate to build a structure lined with a wealth of plants and flowers to celebrate him.

Furthermore, Twyman & Beeching's research suggests that the dome of the Grotto marks out the growing season (March to October) from start to finish, with the top of the shaft acting *"like a pinhole camera, projecting a ball of sunlight onto its north wall"*, the ball varying in size according to the point in the season. At the spring equinox, it sits at the top of the vertical stripe on the wall. It progresses down two central shells of the vertical stripe per week, becoming larger and reaching its maximum size and depth at the summer solstice. Afterwards, it climbs back up at the same rate, diminishing in size, until it shines at the top again at the autumn equinox.

The early May
midday sun
in the dome

Glenn E. Markoe's work on the Phoenicians emphasises the fact that *"the cultic calendars of the various Phoenician cities were governed by a prescribed series of feasts and celebrations that revolved around the agricultural cycle."*

Twyman and Beeching also claimed that the sun at the summer solstice would have been reflected through the opening above the entrance archway to the serpentine passage onto the hearts within the passage (which, uniquely in the structure, were composed of a reflective stone rather than of shells), crisscrossing the passage in this way until the sunlight shone into the 'altar' niche in the end chamber.

Moreover, Melqart was one of the Middle Eastern life-death-rebirth gods. The first recognisable image one sees from the entrance passage is that of a womb and umbilical cord in the left-hand passage. If one takes the right-hand passage around the rotunda, there are phallic symbols in the same position high on the left-hand and right-hand walls. As D. Mitchell has observed, the Shell Grotto could well be seen to represent the journey of the human soul down the birth canal (the original narrow entrance passage) into life and fertility (the images around the rotunda), then on into death (the serpentine passage images) and rebirth among the stars (in the end chamber). There are also two panels in the Grotto which can be interpreted as representing the tree of life, a common symbol for all ancient cultures, as well as one with a date palm sacred to Astarte, the principal Phoenician goddess, probably the origin of the Carthaginian Tanit.

Womb and umbilical cord (?) in the eastern passage of the rotunda

One of the phallic images in the western passage of the rotunda

Why use shells for the designs in the underground temple? John Wilfrid Jackson informs us that shells have been regarded since Ancient Times as *"the source of life, the parent of mankind, the dwelling-place of the deity who conferred the blessings of fertility, not only to mankind, but also to his crops"*. The Phoenician sea people were famous for their shell industry, especially the purple dye they made from murex shells.

It is worth noting here that the flat winkle shells not local to Kent are found in abundance in Cornwall, where the Phoenicians sourced the tin they are thought to have shipped to the Continent via Thanet.

The Phoenician theory thus appears to satisfy our first four criteria, although it has still to be established that these people had a trading post in Margate and therefore the opportunity to build the Grotto. Our sixth criterion is perhaps the most persuasive for this theory. The iconography of the shell designs is highly reminiscent of Phoenician art. The ubiquitous flowers of the Margate Grotto are found on stelae, statues and jewellery. Sabatino Moscati, an expert on the subject, also talks of the Phoenician *horror vacui*: any empty spaces were filled with decoration, usually rosettes. This reminds us that the Shell Grotto seems overladen with all kinds of flowers filling every space between panels, around arches and on ceilings. Particularly striking is the similarity between a star surrounded by rosettes from the Ugaritic culture (which preceded the Phoenicians in Canaan) and the stars in the end chamber of the Grotto.

A Phoenician figurine note the profusion of flowers on the headdress

Passage ceiling – note how all empty spaces are filled with flowers

Ugaritic jewellery, 14th-15th c. BCE

Panel 83 in the Margate Grotto

The star on the right has eight points rather than six, but is otherwise strikingly similar in all its details to the one on the left. The eight-pointed star goes right back to the first civilisations of Mesopotamia, where it symbolised the goddess Inanna, Queen of Heaven. It continued as the symbol of the Queen of Heaven in later Near Eastern religions and represented the goddess Astarte for the Phoenicians.

This same eight-pointed star is also present in two tantalising images we have from the so-called Lupercal discovered on the Palatine Hill in Rome in 2007, while restoration work was taking place on the palace above, the Domus Livia, home of the wife of Augustus, first emperor of Rome. A cavity opened up in the floor of the ruined building, revealing a grotto 8m deep lying 16m underground. It is decorated with shells, mosaics and marble. However, the grotto could only be studied with endoscopes and scanners as fears were high that the space could collapse and damage the ruins above. The only two images we have show striking similarities to those in the Margate Grotto and have been decisively identified as Punic (Phoenician/Carthaginian) by Phoenician specialist, Robert Kerr, who has also described the Margate images as 'unambiguously Punic'.

The ceiling of the Roman grotto under the Domus Livia on the Palatine Hill www.bibliotecapleyades.net/arqueologia/romecave.htm
The Margate grotto almost certainly had a similar vaulted ceiling, later demolished (see p.14).

In addition to the eight-pointed star, the diamond shape with concavely curved sides is ubiquitous in both Margate and Rome. This four-pointed star was the symbol of the ancient Mesopotamian sun god Shamesh, twin brother of Inanna. Their equivalents in Phoenician/Carthaginian

31

religion were Ba'al Hamon and Astarte/Tanit. However, the Carthaginians also had a goddess of the sun called Shapash – perhaps the four-pointed star was her symbol, too.

Theo Vennemann, the linguist who has convincingly argued that the name of the Isle of Thanet, where Margate lies, is derived from the name of the Carthaginian goddess Tanit, is also persuasive in his claim that the name of Rome is derived from Phoenician, the language of Carthage, and that the city was founded by Carthaginians. He argues convincingly that the so-called Lupercal in the Palatine Hill, supposedly the cave where legend has it that a she-wolf suckled the twins Romulus and Remus, future founders of Rome, was a Carthaginian sanctuary, its walls lined with shells. It is remarkable that the two images we have from the cursory examination of its dome done in 2007 bear such a resemblance to some of the shell mosaic in Margate.

Detail of the ceiling www.bibliotecapleyades.net/arqueologia/romecave.htm

The identical four-pointed shape in Margate as in the cave in Rome

A sentence from V.Gordon Childe's Progress and Archaeology also contributes to the thesis that the Margate Grotto is of ancient origin. Writing about the oldest cities in the Tigris-Euphrates delta from the fourth and fifth millennia BCE, Childe states: *"These early temples were already decorated with reliefs in stucco and inlays in shell and imported wood, and furnished with altars for offerings and pediments for cult-images."*

The pediment in the end chamber, which was matched on the opposite wall by another pediment before that area of the Grotto was destroyed by a bomb in the Second World War

Conan and Nellie Shaw, writing in the 1950s, considered the Shell Grotto a site created by Pythagoreans, whose beliefs stemmed from the sixth-century-BCE Greek philosopher Pythagoras. Although remembered today chiefly for his mathematical theories, Pythagoras also preached the transmigration of souls, and held that numbers constitute the true nature of things. The Shaws found great significance in various numerical values in the Grotto shellwork and believed that they reflected the teachings of Pythagoras coming to Margate through the Phoenicians.

Another piece of information about this site which indicates a prehistoric date for its creation is the presence of an anomaly under the end chamber floor. This has variously been described as 'hot rocks' by a geophysical report (unusual in chalk but possibly fragments of a meteorite) and as a vortex by dowsers who pointed to the same area. Many ancient sacred structures are associated with meteorites or sacred stones, most notably the cult centre of Iunu/Heliopolis in Ancient Egypt, the Temple of Apollo at Delphi and the Ka'aba in Mecca. When the Romans dedicated a temple to the Anatolian Mother Goddess Cybele in their capital, they imported the large black meteorite from Phrygia by which she was represented and apparently made it the face of her statue in the temple.

It is important that the Phoenicians represented divinity with non-figural symbols, especially stones. The 'altar' niche in the Grotto bears a resemblance to the cult cart of the Phoenician goddess Astarte, in which a sacred stone called a baetyl was carried. The word baetyl traces back to

Aramaic *be'tel*, meaning 'house of god'. Some baetyls had magic power and the gift of prophecy; their utterances were based on the authority of mighty gods. This would fit in with the Grotto functioning as an oracle cave.

Reverse of Phoenician coin showing a sacred stone (baetyl)
(http://www.forumancientcoins.com/ numiswiki/view.asp?key=baetyl)

The much-damaged 'altar' panel in the end chamber – does it represent a baetyl?

It is said that the bones of a turtle were found when the east wall of the Grotto chamber was destroyed by a bomb in World War II. Large quantities of turtle and tortoise bones were found at the great ceremonial complex at Heirakonpolis in Upper Egypt, although they were not listed as creatures for sacrifice. Whatever may be drawn from turtle bones allegedly found in the Grotto, it is clear that such creatures are much more associated with a Mediterranean culture than a British one. The same is true of the lotus, considered by many to be represented in the shell designs. This is a flower not found in the British Isles in the past. Since it closed at night and sank into the water, re-emerging the following morning, it was a symbol of death and rebirth for the Ancient Egyptians and probably for the Phoenicians, for it seems to be associated with their life-death-rebirth god Melqart.

A lotus flower
(www.freebeautifulpictures.com)

A lotus flower in the Margate shell designs?

We mentioned above that the Phoenician/Carthaginian goddess, Tanit, may well have given her name to the Isle of Thanet, on which Margate lies. Tanit means 'snake goddess'; the snake-like designs in the Shell Grotto could be seen as relevant here. The serpentine passage in the Grotto then also acquires extra significance.

Further corroboration for the Phoenician theory is provided by the hearts in the serpentine passage. The heart was the symbol of the soul in Ancient Egypt and probably in the Phoenician culture. It was weighed against a feather after death to judge how good a life its owner had lived. The same passage also has a figure resembling a skeleton, a symbol of death.

 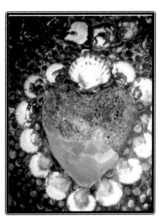

One of the 'snake' panels in the Margate Grotto

One of the hearts in the serpentine passage

The final chamber is full of symbols of the heavens: the sun, moon and stars. The symbol of the setting sun is prominent here. One of the aspects of the principal Phoenician god Ba'al was as the ram-horned god of the setting sun. The Aries symbol of the ram's horns has also been identified in several places in the passages.

The setting sun in the 'altar' niche

It is certainly tempting to conclude that the whole Margate structure represents the human journey, squeezing down the birth passage, through life into adulthood and fertility, towards death and becoming part of the wider universe.

An alternative, or perhaps complementary theory, might see the Grotto as representing the Garden of Eden. As well as the account of Eden found in the Book of Genesis, the Bible has an apparently earlier reference to the Garden in Ezekiel 28:12 & 13. Here it is claimed that the King of Tyre has *"been in Eden the garden of God"*. Tyre was the capital of the Phoenicians and their god Melqart was King of the City.

Perhaps the Grotto represents the Garden of Eden in all its fecundity, complete with snakes, worshipped by this culture as well as by the Israelites. According to Dr Francesca Stavrokopoulou, the Genesis account of Eden involving Adam and Eve is a later story, only inserted in the first chapter of what became the Old Testament in the sixth century BCE.

(http://www.palestineheritage.org/TC-Bethlehem.htm)
Woman's jacket (*taqsireh*) from Bethlehem. Note the designs on the front and the rosettes along the shoulders. Perhaps they hark back to Canaanite (Phoenician) times. Compare them with those in a typical shell panel from the Grotto on the right.

A recurring image in Turkish embroidery above. Part of southern Turkey probably fell within Phoenicia. Note the similarity with the design in the Shell Grotto on the right, often confused with the Egyptian *ankh* sign shown below with its short, straight arms.

ankh

An interesting factor for future study is the acoustics of the Grotto, which are remarkable, and conceivably have some connection with the fact that many shells, especially the background flat winkles, are placed with their underside visible. For example, a whisper into the wall at the central dome can be distinctly heard at the entrance to the end chamber, all the way down the serpentine passage.

Does the placement of shells with the underside visible affect the acoustics of the Grotto?

If we combine these unusual acoustics with the hollow spaces discovered behind the 'altar' and adjoining panel, the parallel with the oracle cave in Gadir is striking. Oracles were often pronounced by a disembodied voice, apparently from a niche.

Conclusions

Considering the results of applying our six criteria to the various theories about the Grotto, there are substantial grounds to support a Phoenician origin. Clearly, we must consider whether a person or persons unknown in more modern times could have built the Grotto to make it appear Phoenician. Although there have been fashions for Classical art, Turkish styles, *chinoiserie* and other exotic forms in Britain over the centuries, the first study of the Phoenician world did not make its appearance until the end of the nineteenth century. Furthermore, the received idea of the culture was for many years that which came down to us from the Greeks and Romans, portraying them as perfidious merchants only interested in making profits. It was claimed that their art was of poor quality, lacked originality and was derivative of the Ancient Egyptians and Greeks. Their greatest contribution to Western European civilisation – the alphabet – was not even universally acknowledged. The first History of Phoenicia was a work by Canon George Rawlinson published in 1889; no serious excavation of the Phoenicians' chief city of Tyre was done before 1973. It therefore seems unlikely that anyone in the millennium before 1838 would have used Phoenician iconography to create the Shell Grotto in Margate. This would indicate that it was actually made in Antiquity.

Yet there has clearly been intervention in the site, probably during the 1820s to the late 1830s. We have already mentioned that the pointed archway in the end chamber dates from the nineteenth century (see p.14), as do the mortar samples from the front of five panels taken in 2009 (see p.13).

The most likely explanation for the facts at our disposal appears to be that the original structure was discovered by George Bowles and/or his neighbour, Captain Easter, between 1824 and 1835. Alternatively, Bowles may only have discovered the underground structure when digging the foundations for the house he started building on the site in 1830. Interestingly enough, these just miss encroaching on the end chamber. Perhaps this was not by design but by chance; it may have remained hidden during his ownership of the property. James Newlove would then have been the first to explore the site and do repairs to the shellwork before opening the site to the public.

Sonia Overall has written a novel about the Shell Grotto entitled The Realm of Shells. She clearly did extensive research and based her plot around Captain Easter carrying out a treasure hunt in the ancient place and destroying the original shell panels.

Whoever was responsible, the gap between the bottom of the shellwork and the floor of the Grotto indicates that the original flooring was probably stripped out; perhaps it was made of valuable material such as marble. The shell designs on the walls and ceilings could, of course, have been recorded in drawings or sketched on slate panels like those seen at Thomas Bowles's home (see p.9) before being removed to search the walls for treasure. The original mosaic could then have been faithfully recreated using the drawings.

Note the gap between the bottom of the shellwork and the floor.

The fact that certain sections of the shellwork were of inferior quality compared with the rest suggests that this may well have been the case. This particularly applied to the area around the 'altar', where we know for a fact that the shellwork was removed and investigations carried out in the 1940s (see p.15). Recent conservation work has much improved "substandard" areas of the mosaic.

In the end, perhaps we should attribute Thomas Bowles's claim to have had a hand in building the Grotto with his brothers as a case of 'sour grapes'. If George Bowles had never discovered the Grotto below his property, it would be understandable that his brother might want to diminish the importance of the discovery by James Newlove, the tenant in the house that George built and a complete newcomer to Margate. It is also common for people to exaggerate the achievements of their ancestors; indeed, any story tends to be embellished each time it is told. The tale handed down in the Bowles family over the years acquired a large number of details which are shown to be incorrect from the evidence of parish records and passenger lists.

As stated at the beginning of this booklet, a definite conclusion about when, why and by whom the Margate Shell Grotto was built will always elude us unless new evidence emerges. If its origins are in modern times, it is certainly strange that no verifiable claim has been forthcoming over the last two centuries.

Many of us would, of course, like it to be an ancient structure, the identity of its exotic builders lost in the mists of time, if only for the thrill of knowing we are visiting a site with a long history. That said, the parallels between the tantalising images of the Rome grotto and the Margate one *do* lend considerable credence to a Phoenician/Carthaginian origin.

Whatever the truth of the matter, the Grotto will remain a fascinating and awe-inspiring place, its beauty only heightened by the enigma of its origins.

Bibliography

Aubet, Maria Eugenia (1994) *The Phoenicians and the West - Politics, Colonies and Trade* (English translation of second edition 2001), Cambridge University Press

BBC website, Tuesday 20 November 2007, *Unearthed... Mythical Roman Cave*, www.bibliotecapleyades.net/arqueologia/romecave.htm

Bolton, Margaret (2007) *The Isle of Thanet – Its History, People and Buildings*, lulu.com (The author has confused the Shell Grotto in Margate with a small basement grotto in a house leased by a Mr Oldfield on what is now Albert Terrace near the Clock Tower.)

Books LLC (2010) *Phoenician Language*, Memphis, Tennessee

Bridgewater, Howard (1948) *The Grotto*, Rydal Press, Keighley, Yorks; 1957 edition by Kent Archaeological Society

Childe, V. Gordon (1944) *Progress and Archaeology*, Watts & Co.

Coates, Richard (2010) "A Glimpse through a Dirty Window into an Unlit House: Names of some North-West European Islands" http://pi.library.yorku.ca/dspace-jspui/bitstream/10315/3642/1/icos23_228.pdf

Comprehensive Gazetteer of England and Wales, The (1894-5), UK Genealogy Archives, www.uk-genealogy.org.uk/england/Kent/towns/Margate.html

Corkhill, W.H. (date unknown) *Avebury, Coldrum and Margate*, Harper Cory Publications Ltd, Ramsgate

Correlli, Marie (1885) "One of the World's Wonders" in *Temple Bar, A London Magazine for Town and Country Readers*, Vol.74, pp.396-401

Cory, Harper (1949) *The Goddess at Margate*, printed by Henry Burt & Son Ltd, Bedford

Daniell, L. S. (1844) *Manuscript Diary of a Journey from London to Paris via Thanet and Folkestone*, Kent History and Library Centre, James Whatman Way, Maidstone, ME14 1LQ, U2666

Dermott, N. (2006) "This far-eastern corner of England (The Isle of Thanet) is determinedly, and widely, exotic", Sandwich Society Magazine

Fanthorne, Lionel & Patricia (1999) *The World's Most Mysterious Places*, Hounslow Press

Goddard, Algernon (1893) *The Mystery of a Margate Catacomb, The Light from Modern Research*, Grottoes and Castles, Margate Grotto Condition Survey, Appendix II, Item 1, 2000, Shell Grotto Archive

Green, Dr Caitlin (2015) "Thanet, Tanit and the Phoenicians: Place-Names, Archaeology and Pre-Roman Trading Settlements in Eastern Kent?" https://www.caitlingreen.org/2015/04/thanet-tanit-and-the-phoenicians.html

Guy, John (1982) "Margate Grotto - Folly or Ancient Shell Temple?" in *Bygone Kent*, Vol.3, No.7, Meresborough Books

Haslam, Ruby (2009) *Reality and Imagery,* Athena Press

Headley G. & W. Meulenkamp (1999) *Follies, Grottoes and Garden Buildings,* Aurum Press Ltd

Hillier, Caroline (1982) *The Bulwark Shore - Thanet and the Cinque Ports,* A Paladin Book, Granada Publishing

Jackson, Hazelle (2001) *Shell Houses and Grottoes,* Shire Album 398, Shire Publications Ltd

Jackson, John Wilfrid (1917) *Shells as Evidence of the Migration of Early Culture,* Manchester at the University Press and Longmans, Green & Co., London

Jones, Barbara (1974) *Follies & Grottoes,* Constable, London

Jones, Barbara (1979) "Some medieval and eighteenth century curiosities and utilities" in *Subterranean Britain - Aspects of Underground Archaeology,* ed. Harriet Crawford, John Baker, London

Khandro.Net (1998-2014) http://www.khandro.net/animal_turtle2.htm

Knight, Charles, London, Publisher (undated c.1847) *The Land We Live In* Volume I, Chapter X, "The Isle of Thanet" (author unknown) p.152 and reprinted (1853) in *Knight's Tourist Companion Through The Land We Live In,* publisher unknown, OCR reprint of original (2009)

LeGear, R.F. (2007) "The Margate Shell Grotto", Kent Archaeological Society, Article 023

Markoe, Glenn E. (2005), *The Phoenicians*, The Folio Society, London

McKinley, Jacqueline I., Matt Leivers, Jörn Schuster, Peter Marshall, Alistair Barclay & Nick Stoodley (2014) *Cliffs End Farm, Isle of Thanet, Kent: A mortuary and ritual site of the Bronze Age, Iron Age and Anglo-Saxon period with evidence for long-distance maritime mobility*, Wessex Archaeology Report 31, Wessex Archaeology

Mitchell, D. (1951) *The Ancient Shell Temple of Margate, also known as The Grotto,* Cooper The Printer Ltd, Margate

Mitchell, C.A. (1949?) *The Grotto - A Study of One of the First Great Civilizations*, Cooper The Printer Ltd, Margate

Moody, Gerald (2008) *The Isle of Thanet from Prehistory to the Norman Conquest*, The History Press

Moscati, Sabatino (ed.) (2000) *The Phoenicians*, Rizzoli International Publications

Museum of London Archaeology (2010), <u>Arlington Square, All Saints' Avenue, Margate – Archaeological desk-based assessment</u>

Newman, John (Third Edition 1983) *North East and East Kent*, The Buildings of England Series, Founding Editor: Nikolaus Pevsner, Penguin Books Ltd, Harmondsworth, Middlesex

Overall, Sonia (2006) *The Realm of Shells,* Fourth Estate, London

Pearson, Chris (2013) *The Shell Grotto And The Mosaic Fountains Found In Houses In Pompeii*, Shell Grotto Archive, Margate

Pearson, Chris (2014) *The Missing "Grotto" Buddha*, Shell Grotto Archive, Margate

Pennick, Nigel (1981) *The Subterranean Kingdom,* Turnstone Press Ltd

Perkins, David (1999) <u>A Gateway Island</u> (unpublished PhD thesis, University College, London)

St Blaise (2009) <u>Condition Survey & Report on The Shell Grotto, Margate</u> for Mr Roger Turner and Ms Sarah Vickery

Scurrell, David (1982) *The Book of Margate,* Barracuda Books

Shaw, Conan and Nellie I. (1954) *The Shell Temple of Margate - An Archaic Masterpiece*, Cooper The Printer, Margate

Smart, Ninian (1989) *The World's Religions,* Cambridge University Press

Stavrokopoulou, Dr Francesca (2011) *The Bible's Buried Secrets - 3. The Real Garden of Eden*, BBC 2 TV series

Strabo, *The Geography of Strabo*, translated by Horace Leonard Jones, Vol.III, Book V, Bibliolife LLC (2009)